HAGGADAH ASK A QUESTION

BY RON ISAACS

ILLUSTRATED BY AMITAI NELKIN

The L'Chayim Library
An imprint of Higher Ground Books & Media

Published by
The L'Chayim Library
An imprint of Higher Ground Books & Media
Springfield, Ohio
www.highergroundbooksandmedia.com

ISBN (Paperback): 978-1-971959-00-9

Printed in the United States of America 2026

For Rabbi Bill and Bev Lebeau who are known for their question-filled seders.

The finest quality of the human being is asking questions.
(Solomon Ibn Gabirol)

Preface

Everyone asks questions. For Jews, asking questions is a national pastime. Questioning can often lead to discovery. Even our holiest biblical books are filled with questions. The Five Books of Moses emphasize the fact that children must ask questions. In Exodus 12:26-27 it says: "And when your children ask you, 'What does the ceremony mean to you?' then tell them, 'It is the Passover sacrifice to the Lord, who passed over the houses of the Israelites in Egypt and spared our homes when He struck down the Egyptian.'" Another verse (Exodus 13:14) states "In days to come, when your son asks you, 'What does this mean?' say to him, 'With a mighty hand the Lord brought us out of Egypt, out of the land of slavery'."

Later in the Bible another passage speaks of a question asked by a child: "In the future, when your son asks you, 'What is the meaning of the stipulations, decrees and laws the Lord our God has commanded you?' tell him: 'We were slaves of Pharoah in Egypt, but the Lord brought us out of Egypt with a mighty hand." (Deut. 6:20-21) This passage as well as the one above have become famous because of their appearance in the Haggadah on Passover. They are the four children: one wise, one wicked, one rebellious, one simple and one who does not even know how to ask a question. Reading them together, the ancient rabbinic sages came to the conclusion that children should ask questions, and it is the duty of parents to encourage their children to ask questions.

Some scholars have even said that faith itself is based on asking questions. "Shall the Judge of all the Earth not do justice?" asked Abraham. "Why, Lord, have you brought trouble on this people?" asked Moses. The great sages of Jewish tradition ask every conceivable question about every conceivable topic. In many Jewish day schools and yeshivahs the headmasters often report that their highest accolade is to ask a good question.

Children love to ask questions. I know, because since 1975

as a congregational rabbi I have entertained a variety of questions that came directly from my students. On a monthly basis, teachers would invite me to their classes for the "Ask the Rabbi" session and I was amazed at the breadth and depth of the queries I received. They also enjoyed telling riddles and being asked riddles. Riddles challenge learners to think critically and creatively.

I received my doctorate from Columbia University in educational gaming and I have studied the impact that learning games can have on educational outcomes. My interest in instructional games and having published several Passover Haggadahs have led to the idea of this book-- Haggadah Ask a Question: Riddle Jokes for the Passover Seder. I have field-tested many of the riddle jokes at my own Passover seders and participants have told me how much they enjoyed them. (Participants were afforded an opportunity to ask the riddle joke questions allowing for even more participation). And at our seder, participants also were given a chance to offer their own punny answers. It made for a more lively and participatory seder. In this book each part of the seder will present riddles related specifically to its theme. To introduce the questions, I have also included a brief explanation of each of the parts of the seder.

I hope that by asking the joke riddles in this book that you will bring joyous smiles to your Passover seder. Wishing you a Happy Passover and as a frog would say—a ribbeting seder!

INTRODUCING HAGGADAH ASK A QUESTION:

RIDDLE JOKES FOR THE PASSOVER SEDER

Everyone asks questions. I always enjoyed listening to my students' questions. I also have received an enormous number of Passover questions from adults, and in particular those regarding the laws of foods that are permitted to be eaten on Passover. Passover, also known as the Festival of Freedom, is the celebration of the Israelites' freedom from Egyptian slavery. As slaves, the Israelites were not permitted to ask questions. To commemorate the Exodus from Egypt story, the rabbis composed the Haggadah, a small book that is read aloud at the seder, the festive meal celebrated on the night of Passover.

The Hebrew word "seder" actually means order. It is called this because the meal is done in a particular order which takes participants from slavery to freedom. The Haggadah is a Hebrew word that means "the telling." It explains the foods on the seder plate, recounts the highlights of the Exodus, and includes songs, prayers and of course questions.

Perhaps the most famous question in the Haggadah is the "Ma Nishtana", which begins "Why is this night different from all other nights." Reading the Haggadah aloud fulfills the Bible's command to all fathers to tell their children the story of the liberation from Egyptian slavery. (Exodus 13:8, 14-15)

The Haggadah is the most widely reprinted book in Jewish history. Well over 2000 editions have been published. As a congregational rabbi, my families were constantly asking me for ideas that would help to enliven the telling of the story. I often used games during the seder, as well as many props and interesting questions. Occasionally I would also resort to riddles and humor.

The Jewish people also have a long tradition of humor. The fourth-century rabbi known as Rabbah delivered his lectures in a serious frame of mind but would always preface them with a joke or witticism, believing that by making his students smile he would help them to better appreciate the complicated subjects he intended to teach. Today, Jewish comics dominate the comedy profession. Even God is said to have a sense of humor, as the Psalmist reminds us: "The one who sits in Heaven shall laugh." Since we are to emulate God in all of God's attributes, why not laugh along with the Holy Blessed One?

A Talmudic legend (Taanit 22a) tells of Elijah, who has a cup of wine waiting for him at every Passover seder. Elijah points out to a rabbi two men who were assured of a place in the World to Come. When the rabbi asked them the nature of their occupation, they said that they were comedians who brought cheer into the lives of those suffering by amusing them with their witticisms.

The Passover Seder is meant to be low-key and fun. Questions are welcomed and a lighthearted spirit is in order. After all, we are celebrating that we are not slaves anymore! At the seder we can rejoice, take our time, and ponder the questions of freedom and service to God.

The *Haggadah Ask a Question* offers more than 250 open-ended riddle jokes specifically related in theme to each of the fifteen different parts of the seder. They are intended to add fun and smiles during the seder. The seder leader is free to pick and choose from among the riddles. There are many benefits to riddles that have no right or wrong answer. The riddles can help tap into the imagination, be creative and empower participants to express themselves, which builds self-confidence in sharing one's thoughts. Unlike trivia questions whose answers must be factual to be correct, the seder leader has the option to suggest to participants a chance to offer their own creative comedic answers (using their wit, puns, and the like) to help bring a smile to all participants. Participants can even choose to vote each time for whose answer they think is best. The seder leader can also choose to go around the table and allow participants an opportunity to ask one of the riddle questions. Keeping points can help determine who becomes the champion of

Haggadah Ask A Question. The author offers his own comedic and punny suggestions answers to each of the joke riddles.

Wishing all who celebrate Passover a spirited, liberating seder with lots of laughter and smiles.

THE SEDER PLATE

The seder plate contains symbolic foods. The *maror* (bitter herbs) symbolize the bitterness of slavery. The *charoset* (mixture of chopped fruits and nuts) symbolizes the mortar used by the Israelites to build the bricks. The *zeroa (shank bone)* and the *beitzah* (roasted egg) symbolize the two sacrifices that were offered on the eve of Passover in the Jerusalem Temple. The *karpas* (green vegetable) symbolizes springtime. The *chazeret* (a bitter herb, usually romaine lettuce) which symbolizes the bitter life of the Israelites in Egypt. Three whole pieces of *matzah* (unleavened bread) are also placed on the seder table, separated by a cloth or napkin. The three pieces represent the ancient Israelite priests, the Levites (assistant priests) and the Israelites. *Matzah* is called the bread of affliction and a reminder of how the Israelites fled Egypt abruptly and did not have time to let their bread rise.

RIDDLES

Why did the seder plate go to therapy?
It couldn't handle all the family drama it was holding.

Why was the seder plate always the life of the party?
It knew how to dish out the best stories with a side of matzah.

Why was the seder plate a detective?
It was always on the case of the missing Afikoman

What did one seder plate say to the other?
Dinner is on me.

What do you call someone who spent hours preparing the seder plate?
Egg-zosted.

Why did the seder plate break up with the matzah?
It said their relationship was too flat.

Why was the seder plate always so calm?
Because it knew how to keep things "plate" and simple.

What do you get when you cross a computer with a seder plate?
A byte of matzah.

Why did the roasted bone break up with the egg at the seder.
Because it said to the egg: "You're too hard boiled for me!"

KADESH
(Blessing the Wine or Grape Juice)

Four cups of wine will be tasted during the seder meal. Each cup is a reminder of one of the promises of redemption in Exodus 6:6-7. The blessing over the first cup at the beginning of the seder meal marks the holiness of the day.

RIDDLES

How can you tell that there are too many people at your seder?
To recline to the left while drinking the wine, you all have to lean in unison.

Why did the man drink 4 cups of Tropicana at his seder?
He couldn't concentrate.

Knock knock.
Who's there?

Leena.
Leena who?
Answer: Leena little closer to the left. We recline at the seder.

What did the grape do when it got stepped on?
It let out a little wine.

Why did the matzah blush during the Kadesh part of the seder?
Because it heard the wine make a grape joke.

Why did the four cups of wine lead the seder in a dance before the Kadesh part of the seder?
Because they wanted to show off their "pour"formance skills.

Why did the wine feel so bubbly at the start of the seder?
Because it was ready to "pour" out its heart to everyone.

What do you call a wine hangover?
The great depression.

How do you decide how much wine to drink?
Take it on a case by case basis.

What do you call a grape that is an anti-diuretic?
Pinot More.

What kind of wine do they serve at the horse races?
Chardon-neigh.

What kind of wine is aged to perfection?
Mos-cat-o.

What kind of wine is known to make you especially drowsy?
Savign-yawn blanc.

What was the name of the crime family that took over the wine importing business?
The Sipranos.

Why did the littlest grape not make it into the wine?
It was pressed into service.

Why did the wine expert insist on drinking from an old tire?
He heard it was a Goodyear.

What is the secret to enjoying a good bottle of wine?
Open the bottle to let it breathe. If it is not breathing, give it mouth-to-mouth.

Do librarians like white wine?
No, they like theirs well-red.

What do you call a wine hangover.
The grape depression.

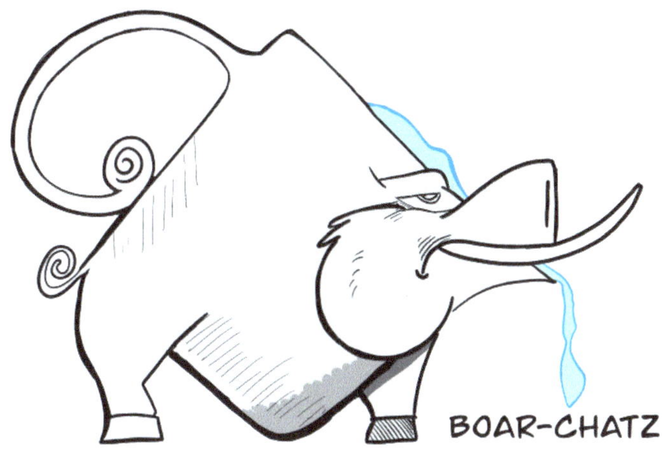

URCHATZ
(Washing Our Hands)

Urchatz is a ritual washing of the hands with a blessing at the beginning of the seder meal.

RIDDLES

Why did the potato go to the sink?
It wanted to be a "clean spud" and wash his hands.

Why did the smart phone go to the bathroom?
Because it heard that there was a "hands-free" handwashing station.

Why did the matzah bring its own towel to "urchatz" during the seder?
Because it didn't want to be "left hanging" when it came time to dry off.

What do you call someone who refuses to wash his hands?
A germinator.

What did one hand say to the other when under the faucet?
"I wash you were cleaner!"

I tried washing my hands without soap. Now my hands are____________
Wet and confused.

KARPAS
(Dipping the Greens)

Seder participants eat a vegetable (often parsley) dipped in saltwater. With this step we combine the hopefulness of spring (represented by the vegetable) with the tears of slavery. (salt water)

RIDDLES

What do you call it when you are dipping parsley in salt water while doing a drive-by?
You're doing a karpas car pass.

Why did the cucumber blush?
Because it saw the salad dressing.

Why did the carrot break up with the broccoli?
Because it found it too stalking.

Why did the karpas blush at the seder?
Because it saw the matzah without its maror.

Why did the karpas bring a map to the seder?
Because it was going on a "dip" tour.

Why did the karpas become a musician?
Because it heard that it could "cello"brate its crunchy tunes at the seder.

Why did the karpas always have a sour attitude?
Because it couldn't handle the "bitter truth" about being eaten.

Why did the karpas jump into the pool?
Because it was sick of dipping in salt water.

Picture a nerdy man named Herb sitting at the Passover table. He asks: "Why must I sit at the kids' table? This really stinks. What is the moral of this story?
No seder would be complete without bitter Herb!

What is the least favorite day of a potato?
Friday.

What do you get when you drop a pumpkin?
Squash.

What is the fastest vegetable of them all?
A runner bean.

What did the mama tomato say to her daughter tomato when out on a jog?
Ketchup.

What vegetable is a sailor's worst enemy?
Leeks.

Why do potatoes always argue?
Because they never see eye to eye.

What is small, red, and whispers?
A hoarse radish.

What did the sweet potato say to the pumpkin?
"I yam what I yam".

What do you call an angry pea?
Grump-pea.

What did one root vegetable say to the other when it misplaced its keys?
I'm sure they'll turnip.

What do you get if you divide the pumpkin by its diameter?
Pumpkin Pi.

What is green and goes to summer camp?
A Brussels scout.

How do you turn soup into gold?
Put 14 carrots in it.

Why did the parsley go to the seder?
It wanted to dip into the conversation.

What did the celery say when it was picked to be the karpas?
"Lettuce romaine calm, it's just a tradition."

Why did the karpas break up with the salt water?
Because things were getting a little too bitter.

YACHATZ (Breaking the Middle Matzah)

Breaking the middle matzah is a reminder of the brokenness that slavery represents. The middle matzah (called the *afikomen*) is wrapped in a cloth in much the same way that Israelites wrapped their baking tools when they quickly left Egypt. It is hidden and participants will be asked to try to find it later in the seder meal.

RIDDLES

How did the matzah do in Vegas?
It was going for broke.

Why did matzah break up with its significant other?
Because it couldn't handle the emotional gluten.

Why did the matzah get a standing ovation at the seder?
Because it really knew how to literally break the mold.

Why did the matzah break up with its partner at the seder?
Because it couldn't handle the pressure of being the "chosen one" in the middle.

Why did the middle matzah go to therapy?
Because it felt so crumby.

What's the hardest part about breaking the middle matzah?
Trying not to crumble under pressure.

What did the middle matzah say when it got broken?
"I knew this was going to be a crack up!"

Breaking the middle matzah is like telling a joke. Why?
It's all about the punch line.

MA NISHTANA: FOUR QUESTIONS

Anyone can ask the four questions, but usually the youngest person if able is asked to lead them. The questions are meant to answer why the night of Passover is different from all other nights of the year.

RIDDLES

Name a question that is often asked at this early stage of the seder.
When can we eat?

What did the child ask at the seder when his mother set the table with new and unusual cutlery?
"Why is this knife different from all other knives?"

A Jew owned two pet rabbis and every so often, he'd give them some cardboard to chew on.
On Passover, he decided to give them some matzah to see how they'd like it.
The two rabbits try the matzah. One said to the other: "Does this cardboard taste a bit funny to you?"
What does this second rabbit respond?
The second rabbit responds: "Not really. Why is this cardboard different from all other cardboards?"

Why did Ma Nishtana refuse to play hide-and-seek during Passover?
Because every time it hid, someone always found it and asked: "Why is this hiding spot different from all other hiding spots?

Why did Ma Nishtana bring a GPS to the seder?
Because it always got lost in the Four Questions and needed directions back to the right page.

What did the matzah say when asked about chanting the four questions?
"I feel a bit flat, but I'm learning to rise to the occasion."

Why did the Four Questions feel nervous?
Because they didn't know the answers.

FOUR CHILDREN

Each person understands things in his or her own way. The four children represent four different responses to the seder and different levels of asking questions. So the seder contains answers to all the ways that questions are asked, whether they be deep and profound or simple. The four children include the wise child, the insensitive child, the uncomplicated child and the young child who is eager to learn but does not yet know enough to even ask.

RIDDLES

The Torah speaks of four types of children who use zoom: the wise, the wicked, the simple and the one who does not know how to mute.

What does the wise son using zoom say?
I'll handle the feature controls and chat room and forward the cloud transcript after the seder.

What does the wicked son using zoom say?
"Since I have limited duration, I scheduled the seder for 5 hours. As it says in the Haggadah, whoever prolongs the telling of the story deserves praise.

What does the simple son using zoom say?
"Hi, am I on? I can see you but I can't hear you."

What does the one on zoom who does not know how to mute say?
"How should I know where I put your keys. I'm stuck in this zoom seder with these fools."

Why did the wise son bring a ladder to dinner?
He hoped it would bring the food to the next level.

Why did the simple son bring a pencil to the bakery?
He thought he needed to draw a loaf of bread.

Where is Putin in the Haggadah?
"Russia, ma hu omer?"

MAGID (The Passover Story)

This part of the seder is the telling of the story of the Exodus from Egypt. Included in this section is the presentation of the ten plagues. It was difficult for Moses to convince Pharaoh to free his people. As a result, God brought ten plagues upon the Egyptians. They included blood, frogs, lice, flies, cattle disease, boils, hail, locusts, darkness and death of the firstborn.

RIDDLES

What kind of shoes did the Egyptians wear during the plague of frogs?
Open-toad.

Why didn't Pharaoh call for help during the second plague?
He had a frog in his throat.

What is the best way to describe Moses and Aaron when the first plague started?
Blood brothers.

What song would have been appropriate to sing to Pharaoh during the seventh plague?
"Hail" to the Chief.

What is the last thing an Egyptian would have ordered for breakfast during the sixth plague?
A hard-boiled' egg.

What dessert might have been served in Egypt during the third plague?
Lice cream.

What type of person does not believe that the main river in Egypt turned to blood?
A "Nile"hist.

Why did the cow refuse to play cards with the other cows?
Because it was afraid of catching "moonia".

Why did the locust get a promotion at work?
It was outstanding in its field.

Why don't beasts get lost?
They always know the beast way around.

Why did the darkness bring a flashlight to the party?
Because it was going to be lit and didn't want to be left in the dark.

What did Moses say to Pharaoh after he refused to let the people go after the first plague.
"That was dumb."

What do you call lice on a bald Pharoah's head?
Homeless.

Why was Pharaoh not able to get his stock broker license?
He was involved in a pyramid scheme.

Why were the Egyptians clapping when the Nile turned to blood.
Because it was B positive.

What did the Egyptian pyramid architects say after frogs fell from the sky.
"Well now there's more green space."

When the plague of boils struck why was it impossible to make a phone call?
Because the service was spotty.

What is Ricky Martin's favorite parody song?
Living Lavita locusts.

What was the cause of the Egyptian baby boom?
Darkness.

What is the name of the Dr. Seuss book that feature the frogs going into the Egyptian slippers?
Frogs in Clogs.

What did the plague of hail say to Pharoah?
"Ice to meet you."

What did Moses say to his brother Aaron when the frogs came down upon the Egyptians?
"Toadily awesome!"

What instrument did the musical play always enjoy playing?
The hopmonica.

Jeopardy Game: Middle East skin plague
Question: What is mid-rash?

What are the top failed Passover promotions?

- U.S. Army
  "The Army of Who Knows One?"

- Animal Awareness Passover Campaign
  "Frogs are our friends, not a plague."

- American Red Cross:
  "This Passover, let's make rivers of blood."

- Adoption Promotion week:

  "Drop your unwanted children in a basket in the NYC reservoir.

- D'Angelo's Barber Shop*:*
  "Free lice check with every haircut

- Republic of China's Population Control Agency:
  "Death of the Firstborn commemorative pins

- Ebay*:*
  "Your afikomen is worth a lot more than that

- Kosher for Passover Ex-Lax:
  "Now in new matzah strength-Ex-dus."

Why did the flies become so popular?
Because they were always buzzing around in Egypt.

Why did the Nile River get so upset?
It just couldn't handle the red tape.

How did the Egyptians react to the hailstorm?
They said: "This is snow joke!"

What do you call a pest that loves to show up with the plagues?
A bug in the system.

What is a Passover frog's favorite game?
Leap of Faith.

What was the favorite tea of Moses?
Libertea

What did the Red Sea say to Moses?
Nothing, it just waved.

What is a frog's favorite Passover song?
Let the Egyptians croak.

Why did the Egyptians comb the desert?
Because there was lice.

When the plague of boils struck why couldn't anyone make a phone call?
The service was spotty.

What song did Pharaoah sing during the Ten Plagues?
Who let the plagues out? Who? Who? Who?

MORE MAGGID

RIDDLES

A little boy once returned from Religious school and his father asked: "What did you learn today?
The boy answered: "The rabbi told us how Moses led the children of Israel out of Egypt."
"How?"
The boy said: Moses was a strong man and he beat up Pharaoh. Then while he was down, he got all the Israelites and asked them to follow him. They all ran toward the sea. When he got there, Moses has the Corp of Engineers build a huge pontoon bridge. Once they got to the other side, they blew up the bridge while the Egyptians were trying to cross. And the Egyptians all drowned." The father was shocked. "Is that what the rabbi taught you?"
What did the boy reply?
"No, but you'd never believe the story he DID tell us!"

If Pharaoh's magicians were to double as fact-checkers, what should they be called?
Sorcerers who source errors.

Why did Moses make Aaron hold the staff?
Because Moses had a staff infection

Which Star War character is the most fascinated by the punishment that the Egyptians received?
Dearth Plagueis

Why did some Hebrews ask their task master for designer work clothes?
They were slaves to fashion.

Where did Moses go when he wanted to exercise with his brother?
He went out for Aa-run.

How do you know when you have too many people at your seder?
When you recite the Ten Plagues, the locusts really ring a bell.

What was the name of the famous secret spy for the Jews in Egypt?
Bondage. James Bondage.

Who is behind Pharoah's evil empire?
Darth Seder.

Knock knock.
Who's there?
Aaron.
Aaron who?
Answer: *Why Aaron you letting the Israelites go?*

Who is the best business woman in the Bible?
Pharaoh's daughter. She pulled a profit out of the water.

Pharaoh walks into a bar. The bartender says: "What's with the heavy heart?
What does Pharoah answer?
Pharoah answers: "I want my mummy."

Moses was sitting in the Egyptian ghetto. Things were horrible. Pharoah would not speak to him. The Israelites were angry and Moses was about ready to give up. Suddenly came a voice from above:
"Moses, Moses, listen to me. I have good news and bad news."

Moses was staggered. The voice continued.
"You Moses will lead the Israelites out of bondage. If Moses refuses, I will smite Egypt with frogs. And if Pharoah continues to block your way, I will smite Egypt with a plague of locusts. And if Pharaoh's army pursues you, I will part the waters and open your path to the Promised Land.
Moses was stunned. That's great God. But what's the bad news?
"You Moses must write the Environmental Impact Statement!"

Why did Pharoah refuse to play cards with Moses?
Because every time Moses got a pair, he'd part the deck.

Why did Pharoah always carry a map?
Because he heard Moses was always making waves at the Red Sea.

Why was Pharoah such a terrible singer?
Because whenever he tried to hit the high notes, Moses kept telling him to let his people go!

How do you measure the length of a seder?
In plagues per hour.

I heard they added a new section to the Passover Haggadah this year. What is it called?
When do we get to eat?

Why did the Israelites run quickly through the parted Red Sea?
Because they didn't want to walk like an Egyptian.

Why did the Israelites wander in the desert for so long?
They lost their Waze.

Why did Moses never get lost in the desert?
Because he always had a staff to guide him.

What are two Paskin-Rabbi's ice cream flavors especially created for Passover?
Manishtana Nut and Mi Kamocha.

What did Pharoah say to the stone statue?
You really know how to rock this place.

What did Moses invent?
He was the first person to download something to a tablet from the cloud.

RACHTZAH (Washing Our Hands)

Rachtzah is the washing of the hands a second time. It is done with a blessing since participants are able to eat more substantial food. The ancient Israelite priests washed their hands before preparing a sacrifice. Through the ceremony of ritual washing of the hands participants symbolically become priests and the seder table becomes the altar.

RIDDLES

Knock knock.
Who's there?
Honey bee.
Honey bee who?
Answer: *Honey bee a dear and bring over a cup for washing our hands.*

Why did rachatza bring a stopwatch to the seder?
Because they wanted to be sure that they didn't spend too much time "rachatz"-ing during the handwashing part.

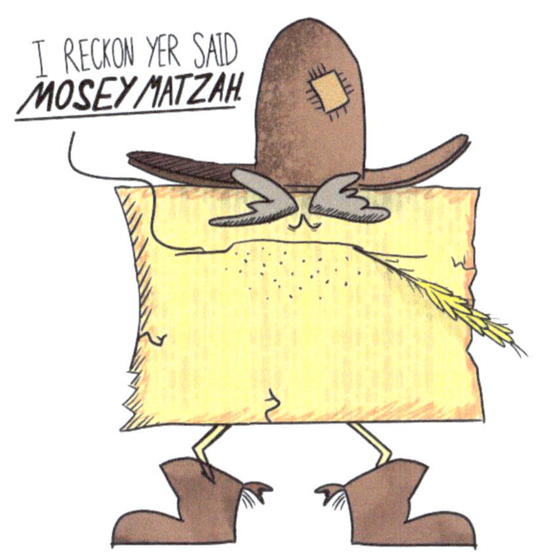

MOTZI MATZAH (Eating the Matzah)

Two blessings are recited before eating the matzah. The blessings show thanks to God for bread (a symbol of all things that we eat on a regular basis) and the matzah which is eaten during Passover.

RIDDLES

What makes a great seder like a piece of matzah?
They both should take less than 18 minutes.

Why did the matzah go to the doctor?
Because he started to feel crumby.

Have I ever told you the joke about matzah and jelly?
I better not because it might spread.

Why did the matzah rob the bank?
He needed the dough.

What do you call someone who derives great pleasure from the bread of affliction?
A matzochist.

Why did the matzah quite his job?
Because he didn't get a raise.

What did the matzah say to the bread?
"Don't worry. I'll cover for you."

Why did the matzah refuse to rise?
It had a yeast infection.

Why did the matzah go to school?
To get a little "bread"ucation.

A matzah walks into a bar. The bartender says: :Haven't seen you in a while. Where have you been?
What does the matzah say?
I've had some bad breaks.

Why was the matzah always so serious?
Because it never cracked a smile!

Why did the matzah feel so crumby?
Because it went through a bad break-up.

Jewish scientists are working on a new matzah creation for Passover.

What is the new matzah's name?
Matzah 2.0 The Unleavened Revolution

The matzah balls were so hard this year that you could use them for______________.
Answer: Golf balls

What is a good deal in a kosher supermarket that you should definitely not pass over?
Free matzahs

Why did the matzah go to therapy?
It had too many unleavened issues.

What did one piece of matzah say to the other?
"You crack me up!"

What kind of music does matzah like?
Music with flat notes.

Why did the matzah bring sunscreen to the seder?
Because it didn't want to get too baked.

Why is the matzah always calm?
Nothing will make it rise.

What did the grape juice say to the matzah?
"You crack me up, but I'll stick by you."

What did the ring announcer say when two matzahs at their boxing match were about to fight each other?
"Let's get ready to crumble."

What is the best way to buy a quantity of matzah?
By a flat rate.

How do you know that it's okay to put garlic on your matzah?
Matzah zo al shoom (Hebrew for garlic) mah.

MAROR (Eating the Bitter Herbs)

The bitter herbs are eaten in order to symbolically taste the bitterness of slavery.

RIDDLES

Bitter herbs walks into a bar. What does the barman say?
Sorry, we don't serve food here.

When it comes to karpas, who is the king of Passover?
Elvis Parsley.

What did the lion say after tasting the bitter herbs?
"Ma-Roar!"

How should you describe an incredibly patriotic child who mistakenly eats both types of horseradish and then starts to cry?
Red, White and Blue.

Where did Moses go when he wanted to exercise with his brother?
He went out for Aa-run.

Why do we eat maror with the four cups?
When it chrains, it pours.

What makes a great seder like a piece of matzah?
They should both take less than 18 minutes.

An advanced class was studying Talmud with a teacher who was less advanced. Their topic was acceptable foods for Passover. The Talmud mentions one food called *tamcha* (a type of bitter herb). One of the students asked, "What is the meaning of *tamcha?"*The teacher, not very sure as to how to translate the word, instructed the student to look it up in the great French commentator Rashi's commentary.

The child did as he was asked. Rashi had written, "This was to be explained later in the chapter." The child turned the pages and saw that the Talmud quotes the cryptic words of a sage who explains that *tamcha* is the same as *temachta.* Again, the child questioned the teacher, "What is *temachta?"*

The teacher responded, "Didn't I tell you to read what Rashi says?"

The student replied: "I did look at the Rashi comment, and he says that *temachta* is the same as the French word *marubiya.* The student, now more puzzled than ever asked again, "But what is *marubiyah?"*

The teacher, exasperated by the child's questions and frustrated by his own ignorance, blurted out...............

"Go ask a Frenchman!"

What is the favorite game of bitter herbs?
Bitter or Better

Why do bitter herbs make for terrible actors?
They also play seasoned characters.

KORECH (Making Hillel's Sandwich)

Participants are invited to eat a sandwich consisting of matzah, bitter herbs and *charoset* (mixture of nuts and fruits). Hillel, an important ancient rabbi taught that eating this type of sandwich is the way that people ate the Passover sacrifice during the time of the ancient Temple.

RIDDLES

Why did the sandwich go to the party?
It wanted to be the toast of the town.

Why did the matzah refuse to be part of the Korech ceremony?
Because it didn't want to be "sandwiched" between the bitter herbs.

What did the maror say to the matzah during Korech?
"You think you're tough
Try being as bitter as me!"

What did the lettuce say to the baguette?
"Hey, I'm on a roll."

What is the best snack for the beach?
A sand-wich.

What do you call a cannibal eating a sandwich?
A sub-human.

What would the population be if the earth were one big sandwich?
In-bread.

What did the sandwich say when it broke up with his bread girlfriend?
"You deserve butter."

Why didn't the sandwich want to stay up late?
It was past its bread time.

What is a deer's least favorite sandwich bread?
Sour doe.

What is a turtle's favorite sandwich?
Peanut butter and jelly fish.

What do you get if you cross a pig and a witch with sand?
A ham sandwich.

What did the sandwich say when it got a new job?
"Lettuce celebrate!"

How do you make a toasted sandwich in the jungle?
Put it under a gorilla.

What do you call a monk who steals a grilled cheese right off the griddle?
Out of the frying pan and into the friar.

What did the caveman order at the café?
A club Sandwich.

What do you call it when you make sandwiches at a sleepover?
Peanut butter and jammies.

What did the movie director say after shooting the last scene and being handed a sandwich?
"That's a wrap."

What did the cop have on his sandwich?
Traffic jam.

What did elves use to make sandwiches?
Shortbread.

What do you get when you eat a sandwich in bed?
Breadcrumbs.

Why do sandwiches like to sit near a fireplace?
They like feeling toasty.

What do you call a pack of sandwiches on a skateboard?
Meals on wheels.

What is a printer's least favorite kind of sandwich?
Paper jam.

What kind of cheese does a guitar enjoy in his sandwich?
String cheese.

What do you call a pun sandwich?
A Punini.

Why did the man leave his sandwich in the elevator at work?
He wanted to take his lunch to the next level.

What did the cannibal serve with tea?
Finger sandwiches.

Why didn't Shakespeare eat chicken burgers?
He was too caught up with Ham-let.

Where do astronauts keep their sandwiches?
In their launch box.

What is a singer's favorite sandwich?
So-la-mi.

Where do sandwiches like to dance?
At a meat ball.

Why was the sandwich in a grumpy mood?
It woke up on the wrong side of the bread.

What did the baker say to his assistant after he caught him stealing money from the till?
This is a breach of crust.

What did the tea say to the matzah.
We're tea-riffic together.

What did the Hillel sandwich say to the brisket?
"Sorry, I'm already wrapped up in another tradition."

What is the Hillel sandwich's favorite type of music?
Heavy matzah.

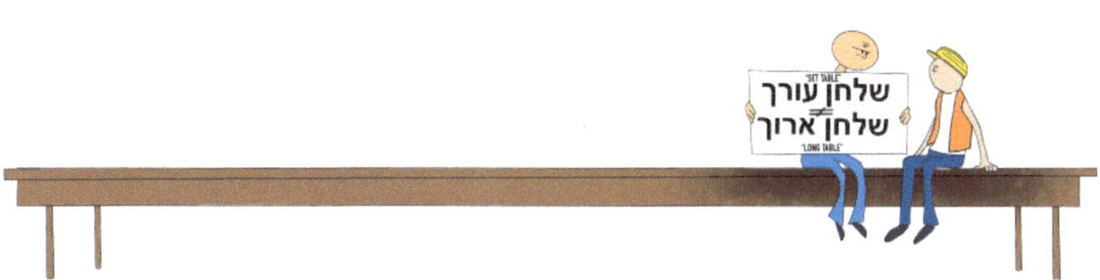

SHULCHAN ORECH (Serving the Meal)

The seder meal often begins with serving an egg because an egg is a symbol of new life. This is the new life the Israelites enjoyed after they were freed from Egypt. Some use hardboiled because the more you boil an egg the harder it gets. The Israelites were the same way. The more that Pharoah punished them, the stronger and more numerous they became.

RIDDLES

What was Aaron's official title?
Chief of Staff.

Why are gold-colored knee-high socks forbidden on Passover?
They create golden calves.

Where does the U.S. military store its chametz?
Fort Leavenworth.

What is the most appropriate meal to serve on Passover to commemorate the Red Sea miracle?
A banana split.

What type of beer did the Egyptians serve to the slaves?
He-brew.

What is the King of Egypt's favorite dish?
Farro.

How many Pharaohs does it take to screw in a light bulb?
One, but he won't let it go.

What's a frog's favorite drink?
Croak-a-cola.

How does NASA organize their Passover seders?
They planet.

Why do we have a seder on Passover?
So we can seder right words.

Why did Pharoah go to therapy?
He had too many pyramid schemes.

What sport did the Israelites play in the desert?
Matzah ball.

Why did some Israelites ask their task masters for designer work clothes?
They were slaves to fashion.

There is a new product available in the Passover aisle this year. It's called Metamatzil.

What do you suspect a good name would be for the logo of this product?
Let My People Go.

How did Passover get its name?
Since people can't often reach the matzah at the seder table, they often can be heard saying "Could you please pass over the matzah?"

Did you hear about the gefilte fish that went deaf?
It had to buy a herring aid.

What is the best way to describe baby Moses' mother after baby Moses was sent floating down the Nile?
She was a basket case.

What did the Hebrew say when Pharaoh declared that they must make bricks without using other materials?
"OK Rameses, now you've gone too far. This is the last straw."

The Jewish nation walks into a bar. Hundreds of thousands of Israelites pile in and out of the bar.
The bartender then says: You thought splitting the sea was hard. Now…………………
Try splitting the check.

What kind of cheese do people love to eat during Passover?
Matzo-rella.

Why wouldn't Moses let anyone use his staff?
He couldn't part with it.

How can you tell that there are too many people at your seder?
While waiting for everyone to wash their hands the second time, the matzah rises.

What did the WiFi network say to the family during Passover?
"Chametz free connection established!"

Why did the app developer enjoy Passover?
Because he could finally appreciate the power of "unleavened" code!

What did the virtual assistant say during the Passover seder?
"I'm sorry, I can't help with that. But I can recite the Four Questions!"

What did the mohel bring to the seder?
A bris kit.

What kind of cake is often served after the Passover meal?
A stomach cake.

A matzah ball walks into a bar. What does the bartender then say:
"Is this round on you?"

How many seders does it take to screw in a light bulb?
Who knows, one?

What's the name of the synagogue of only Jewish democrats in 2026?
B'nai Barak.

Why do Jewish mothers make great parole officers?
They never let anyone finish a sentence.

Why did the Egyptians have all the Jews build the store houses?
Because they were anti-cementic.

What does the bartender say to the kiddush cup when it walks into the bar?
Sorry, we don't serve whiners here.

Why did the mortgage crisis start on Passover?
Too much leaning.

During the splitting of the Red Sea, what diagnosis did Moses receive from his psychiatrist?
He was diagnosed with a split personality.

What are three signs that your seder has too many people?

While waiting for everyone to wash their hands the matzah rises.
When Elijah shows up you give him his wine "to go."
To recline at the dining table everyone has to do it in unison.

What song was sung at the first ever Passover seder at Yankee stadium?
Take Me Out to the Seder.

Why do we especially remember the exodus on the last day of Passover in synagogue?
There is a mass exodus in many shuls.

Why don't they ever play cards at the Red Sea?
Because Moses always splits the deck.

What did Moses say when the Red Sea parted?
"Well, this is a shore thing!"

Why did Moses start a landscaping business after parting the Red Sea?
He was great at clearing paths.

Moses walks into a bar. The bartender says, "What can I get you?" What does Moses reply?
"I'll have a sea breeze, but hold the water!"

What Bible verse gave an inventor the idea to create a matzah cover for a toilet seat?
Let My People Go.

What is a frog's favorite flower?
A croak-us.

T.S.A.-FUN

TZAFUN (Eating the Afikoman)

The *afikomen* is a kind of dessert. In the days of the ancient Temple, the Passover offering was the last thing eaten at the seder. Now that the Temple is gone, the *afikomen* serves as a symbol of the offering. The *afikoman* is the piece of the middle matzah that was broken earlier in the seder and hidden away. Participants are now given time to look for it and often receive a "finder's fee."

RIDDLES

What is the most famous afikomen song?
Afikoman round the mountain when she comes.

What did the teddy bear say when he was offered the afikomen?
No thanks, I'm stuffed.

Why did the afikomen got into therapy?
Because it always felt it was being broken into pieces during the seder.

Why did the afikomen run for office?
Because it wanted to be the undisputed missing piece of the government.

Why did the family finish the seder early?
Because it heard that the afikomen was getting a head start on the dessert.

If Dr. Jekyll finds the afikomen without even trying, who should you blame?
Mr. Hide

What is a pirates favorite part of the seder?
The "aye"-fikoman.

What did the teddy bear say when he was offered a piece of the afikomen?
"No thanks, I'm stuffed."

The good news is that we can't continue with the meal until we find the afikomen. What is the bad news.
"I can't remember where I hid it."

Why did the afikoman go missing?
It kneaded a break!

BARECH (Giving Thanks)

Just as God was thanked for food before the meal was served, God is now thanked after the meal with the traditional Grace after the meal. (Birkat HaMazon)

RIDDLES

Why did the polite diner get mistaken for a detective?
Because after every meal he'd always say: "Thank you for the food. It was so good, it's criminal."

Why did the salad go to etiquette school?
Because it wanted to learn how to properly say: "Thank you for leaf-ing me satisfied after every meal."

ELIJAH AND MIRIAM

According to Jewish tradition, Elijah the Prophet is the one who will announce that the messianic era is coming. Since the seder is a time to celebrate freedom and liberty, there is a tradition that Elijah will visit every home celebrating Passover to witness the celebration and announce the ultimate in freedom and liberty. A special cup of wine is set on the Passover seder table for him.

Miriam, sister of Moses, is also often honored at the seder. A ceremonial cup filled with water is placed on the seder table. It symbolizes Miriam's well which traveled with the Israelites in the desert.

RIDDLES

Knock knock.
Who's there?
Eli Ya.
Eliyah who
Eliyahu HaNavi

Did you hear about the new internet search engine for Passover. It is called…..
eliYahoo

What starchy vegetable did Moses' sister enjoy eating?
Miri-yams.

The Religious school teacher was carefully explaining the story of Elijah and the false prophets of Baal. She explained how Elijah built the altar, put wood on it, cut the steer in pieces and laid it upon the altar. Then Elijah commanded the people of God to fill four barrels of water and pour it over the altar. He had them do this four times.

"Now, said the teacher. Can anyone in the class tell me why God would have Elijah pour water over the steer on the altar?"

A little girl in the back raised her hand and answered:......................................
"To make the gravy!"

Why were the Israelite homes so drafty during Passover?
Because they always left the door open for Elijah.

What was Miriam's first dance after she crossed the Red Sea?
A free's dance.

What did Elijah say when he discovered Uber?
"I'll take a chariot, thank you very much!"

Why did Miriam bring a tambourine to the Red Sea?
She knew it was going to be a rockin' good time.

What did Miriam say when she saw Moses part the Red Sea?
"Well, that's one way to make an entrance!"

What's Miriam's favorite type of music?
Anything that splits the crowd.

Why is Elijah a bad guest?
He always leaves without saying goodbye.

HALLEL (Psalms of Praise)

The Hebrew word *hallel* means "praise." It refers to the name of a group of Psalms (115-118) that the Levites sang in the ancient Jerusalem temple. The Hallel psalms all thank God for the many things that God has done for the Israelites.

RIDDLES

Why did the choir member bring a ladder to synagogue?
Because he wanted to praise God one step higher.

Why did the choir director bring a map to rehearsal?
Because he wanted to be sure he could find the right key to use for praising God.

Why did the rabbi bring a basketball to synagogue?
Because he wanted to "shoot" some praises to the One on High.

Why did the congregants bring a ladder to the synagogue?
Because they wanted to reach even a higher note when praising God.

Why did the choir bring an extra pair of socks to their performance?
Because they were ready to sing their hearts out and didn't want to knock their socks off with heavenly praise.

NIRTZAH (Completing the Seder)

The Passover seder is coming to the end. God is now asked to accept the gifts of thought and feeling that participants have offered. The seder ends with the chanting of the Hebrew words *l'shanah haba'ah b'yerushalayim*—next year in Jerusalem. With these joyful words, participants hope to join with all in a peaceful Jerusalem and a reminder to keep working to make the world a better place.

RIDDLES

Why did the matzah break up with the bread?
Because it said: "Next year in Jerusalem, but the bread was loafing around.

Why did the matzah skip town?
Because it heard "next year in Jerusalem" and decided to get an early start on the journey.

Why did the Haggadah feel relieved when the seder was over?
Because it finally got to close its pages and say: "Phew, that's a wrap. Next year in Jerusalem but for now I'm closing shop.

What is often said after we say at the end of the seder "next year in Jerusalem."
"How about next week with pizza."

Neflix and Yahoo are merging and moving their headquarters to Jerusalem. Guess what they will be called?
Net 'in'Yahoo.

SONGS

Several Passover songs are sung at the end of the Passover seder. The song titled Who Knows One is meant to be funny and humorous, while still imparting important lessons. It is a cumulative song, with each of the thirteen verses built on top of the previous verses. The first verse runs:" Who knows one? I know one. One is our God in heaven and on earth." In a sense one can consider Who knows one a riddle song. Sometimes the song is played as a memory game, recited without looking. Sometimes the goal is to recite the entire verse in one breath. The song clearly demonstrates how everything can and should relate to God: "If I say One', you think God!' If I say 'Five', you think 'Books of Moses.'

Who Knows One

RIDDLES

What do you call numbers always on the move?
Roamin' numerals.

Why did the two fours skip a meal?
Because they already ate.

Everyone knows that 7 ate 9, But why?
Because he needed to eat 3 square meals a day.

Why did Bob quit his job cleaning bathrooms at a hotel that had 288 rooms?
Because it was too gross.

How do you make seven even?
Take away the "s."

Why did the frog have difficulty singing the song Who Knows One?
It was hard for him to count on webbed toes.

Chad Gadya (One Little Goat)

This playful cumulative song is symbolic of the different nations that conquered the Land of Israel. The kid in the song symbolizes the Jewish people; the cat, Assyria; the dog, Babylon, the stick Persia, and so on.

RIDDLES

Why did the two goats start a band?
They had lots of "baaasic" instincts and wanted to make goat music.

Why was the cat sitting on the computer?
He wanted to keep an eye on the mouse.

Why did the dog sit in the shade?
It did not want to be a hot dog.

Why was the stick a great comedien?
It always knew how to "branch out" and make everybody laugh.

Why did the fire refuse to go out?
It heard it was hot stuff and did not want to extinguish its reputation.

Why did the water go to school?
It wanted to be well-rounded and soak up all the knowledge.

Why did the Angel of Death fail as a comedian?
His jokes were a killer but his delivery was deadpan.

Why did the ox go to school?
He wanted to be a "gradu-ox"

Why did the stick break up with the tree?
It found out that the tree was too wooden for its liking.

Why did the butcher quit his job?
He was tired of the daily grind.

If you have a seder night on a large and fancy boat, what song should you sing at the end of the night?
Chad Gad Yacht.

Name a sporty goat's go-to-drink?
Goat-arade.

What is a kid goat's favorite nursery rhyme to sing?
"Row, row row yo*ur goat.*

What is a mountain goat called?
A hillbilly.

What did the goat say about her veggies?
"These are so baaaaad!"

What did the bored goat say?
"Meh!"

What musical do goats watch over and over again?
Joseph and the Amazing Technicolor Dreamgoat.

What do you call a goat that swims really fast?
A motor goat.

What tv show do goats most enjoy watching with their families?
America's Goat Talent.

What do you call a young goat that knows martial arts?
A karate kid.

What is a goat's beard called?
A goatee.

What do goats say when they trick their parents?
"I was just kidding."

What do you call a goat that works in a donut shop?
A battering ram.

What is a napping baby goat called?
A kid-napper.

What did the kid say when he pranked his parents?
Goatcha!

What does a goat say when he has to repeat himself?
"Here we goat again.

Which artists do goats love the most?
Vincent Van Goat.

Why did the goat end up crashing into the wall?
She didn't see the ewe turn.

What is a goat dressed as a clown called?
A silly billy.

What does a goat usually eat for breakfast?
Goat-meal.

About the Author

Ron Isaacs is the spiritual leader of historic Beth Judah Temple in Wildwood New Jersey. He has published more than 160 books. His Passover books for Higher Ground Books and Media include Let's Make a Deal, I am Passover and Seder in the Desert. He has also written several Passover Haggadahs including The Family and Frog Haggadah (co-author Karen Rostoker Gruber) and Seder in Motion: A Haggadah to Move Body and Soul (co-author Leora Isaacs).

About the Illustrator

Amitai Nelkin, originally from Highland Park in Jersey, received his bachelor's degree in biology from Brown University. He is the creator and illustrator behind Shtuyot.org, an online store full of wacky Jewish products. He enjoys bringing his love of illustration, puns and Judaism together.

About This Imprint

The L'Chayim Library is a dedicated imprint of Higher Ground Books & Media focused on publishing works that explore Jewish faith, tradition, scholarship, and spiritual life. Guided by a commitment to accuracy, thoughtful reflection, and meaningful dialogue, the imprint highlights voices that contribute to the understanding and appreciation of Jewish heritage.

Faith Advisor Rabbi Ron Isaacs serves as a subject matter expert for the imprint, helping ensure that titles reflect integrity and authenticity within Jewish thought and practice.

Other titles from Ron Isaacs & Higher Ground Books & Media:

I Want to Meet Elijah by Ron Isaacs

Unstuck by Ron Isaacs

Mystery of the Ram's Horn by Ron Isaacs

Where Are You God? by Ron Isaacs

Seder in the Desert by Ron Isaacs

Let's Make a Deal by Ron Isaacs

The Power of Song by Ron Isaacs

Elsa the Elephant by Ron Isaacs

The Boy Who Opened the Heavens by Ron Isaacs

Here Come the Seagulls by Ron Isaacs

Look to the Birds by Ron Isaacs

Midnight the Holy Cow by Ron Isaacs

The Sheep With the Golden Horns by Ron Isaacs

Song Heard Round the World by Ron Isaacs

Sing to God: Halleluyah! By Ron Isaacs

Moses and the Extra Ten by Ron Isaacs

Prayer for the World: Song of the Grass by Ron Isaacs

Reba Loves Shabbat by Ron Isaacs

I Am Hanukkah by Ron Isaacs

I Am Passover by Ron Isaacs

I Am Purim by Ron Isaacs

Add these titles to your collection today!

http://www.highergroundbooksandmedia.com

HIGHER GROUND BOOKS & MEDIA IS AN INDEPENDENT PUBLISHER

Do you have a story to tell?

Higher Ground Books & Media is an independent Christian-based publisher specializing in stories of triumph! Our purpose is to empower, inspire, and educate through the sharing of personal experiences. We are always looking for great, new stories to add to our collection. If you're looking for a publisher, get in touch with us today!

Please be sure to visit our website for our submission guidelines.

http://www.highergroundbooksandmedia.com/submission-guidelines

HGBM SERVICES IS OUR CONSULTING FIRM

AUTHOR SERVICES

HGBM Services offers a variety of writing and coaching services for aspiring authors! We can help with editing, manuscript critiques, self-publishing, and much more! Get in touch today to see how we can help you make your dream of becoming an author a reality!

*****

We also offer social media marketing services for authors, small businesses, and non-profit organizations. Let us help you get the word out about your book, your projects, and your mission. We offer great rates, quality promos, consistent communication, and a personal touch!

http://www.highergroundbooksandmedia.com/editing-writing-services

Need Bulk Copies?

If you would like to order bulk copies of this book or any other title at Higher Ground Books & Media, please contact us at **highergroundbooksandmedia@gmail.com**.

We offer discounts for purchases of 20 or more copies. Excellent for small groups, book clubs, classrooms, etc.

Get in touch today and get a set of great stories for your students or group members.

www.ingramcontent.com/pod-product-compliance
Lightning Source LLC
LaVergne TN
LVHW052256100826
845147LV00001B/59

9781971959009